Cc

Bela Davis

Abdo
THE ALPHABET
Kids

abdopublishing.com

Published by Abdo Kids, a division of ABDO, PO Box 398166, Minneapolis, Minnesota 55439.
Copyright © 2017 by Abdo Consulting Group, Inc. International copyrights reserved in all countries.
No part of this book may be reproduced in any form without written permission from the publisher.

Printed in the United States of America, North Mankato, Minnesota.

102016

012017

THIS BOOK CONTAINS
RECYCLED MATERIALS

Photo Credits: iStock, Shutterstock

Production Contributors: Teddy Borth, Jennie Forsberg, Grace Hansen

Design Contributors: Christina Doffing, Candice Keimig, Dorothy Toth

Publisher's Cataloging in Publication Data

Names: Davis, Bela, author.

Title: Cc / by Bela Davis.

Description: Minneapolis, Minnesota : Abdo Kids, 2017 | Series: The alphabet |
    Includes bibliographical references and index.

Identifiers: LCCN 2016943883 | ISBN 9781680808797 (lib. bdg.) |
    ISBN 9781680795899 (ebook) | ISBN 9781680796568 (Read-to-me ebook)

Subjects: LCSH: English language--Alphabet--Juvenile literature. | Alphabet
    books--Juvenile literature.

Classification: DDC 421/.1--dc23

LC record available at http://lccn.loc.gov/2016943883

Table of Contents

Claire plays **c**ards.

Cc

Carly eats corn.

Cc

Chris does a **c**artwheel.

Cc

Carlos **c**an play **c**larinet.

Cc

Camila **c**olors in her book.

Cc

Carter and **C**aleb **c**amp.

Cc

Callie **c**uts with **care**.

Cc

Cassie **c**arries a **c**hi**c**ken.

18

Cc

What does **C**ole have?

(**c**ookies)

More Cc Words

camel

carrots

camera

castle

Glossary

care
serious attention applied to
doing something.

clarinet
a woodwind instrument with a
mouthpiece, a tube with a flared
end, and holes stopped by keys.

Index

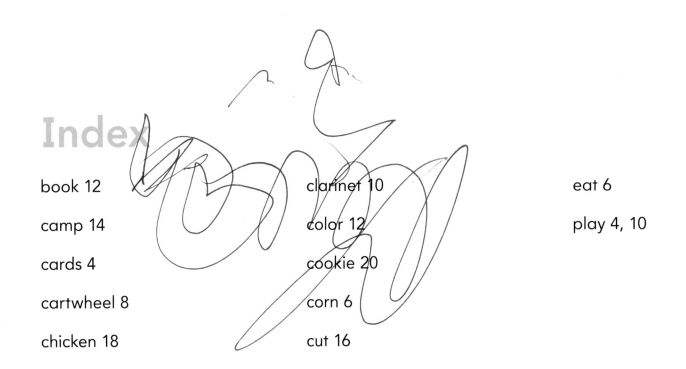

abdokids.com

Use this code to log on to abdokids.com and access crafts, games, videos, and more!

Abdo Kids Code:
TCK8797